EXPLORING
MAGNETISM

Neil Ardley

Series consultant: Professor Eric Laithwaite

Franklin Watts

London   New York   Toronto   Sydney

The author
Neil Ardley gained a degree in science and worked as
a research chemist and patent agent before entering
publishing. He is now a full-time writer and is the
author of more than fifty information books on
science, natural history and music.

The consultant
Eric Laithwaite is Professor of Heavy Electrical
Engineering at Imperial College, London. A well-
known television personality and broadcaster, he is
best known for his inventions on linear motors.

© 1983 Franklin Watts Ltd

First published in Great Britain
1983 by Franklin Watts Ltd
12a Golden Square
London W1R 4BA

First published in the USA by
Franklin Watts Inc.
387 Park Avenue South
New York
N.Y. 10016

Printed in Belgium

UK edition:
ISBN 0 86313 026 7
US edition:
ISBN 0–531–04617–6
Library of Congress Catalog
Card No: 82–62993

Designed by
David Jefferis

Illustrated by
Janos Marffy
Hayward Art Group
Arthur Tims

ACTION SCIENCE

EXPLORING MAGNETISM

Contents

Equipment

You will need several magnets to carry out all the activities in this book. There should be at least two bar magnets, and preferably a horseshoe magnet and a few small magnets.

In addition to magnets and several everyday objects and materials, you will also need the following equipment.

Aluminum foil	File (large)	Matchboxes
Ball bearings	Insulated wire	Paper clips
Cork	Lampholder and bulb	Rusty can
Dry battery (about 4.5 volts)	(same voltage as dry battery)	Scissors (large steel pair)
		Screw (medium)

Introduction

Nothing is more mysterious in science than
magnetism. The way in which a magnet can
move an object that is some distance away
looks like magic. In fact, no one really
knows why magnets behave in this way.
But we are able to put magnetism to use in
many machines. Without magnetism we
would have no television, for example, no
record or cassette players, no telephones,
and no computers.

By doing the activities in this book, you
will discover the ways in which magnets
behave. Among the experiments are some
which show odd and unexpected things
that magnets can do. Other activities
explore the Earth's magnetism and
investigate the use of electricity to produce
magnetism.

Take care of your magnets. Dropping
magnets may cause them to lose their
magnetism. Don't worry about leaving
magnets clustered together as this does
no harm.

✸ This symbol appears throughout the
book. It shows you where to find a
scientific explanation for each activity.

Magnetic materials

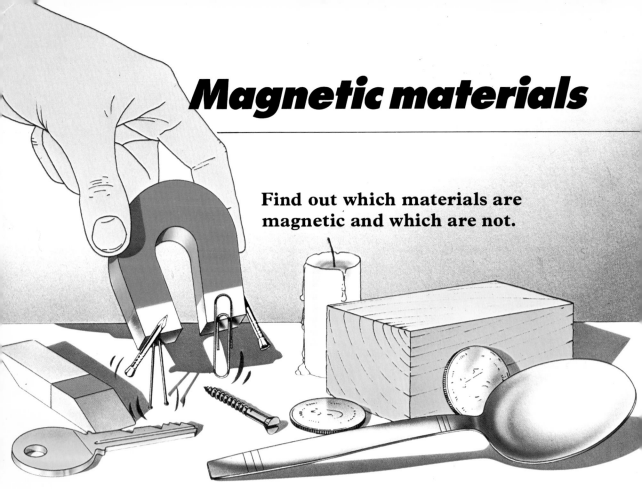

Find out which materials are magnetic and which are not.

△ The magnet does not attract objects like an eraser or pieces of paper because they are not made of metal. It does not pick up metal objects like coins or silver cooking foil, either. This is because the coins and foil are made of non-magnetic metals like copper and aluminum.

Test for magnetism

Make a pile of different objects. Use pins, nails, paper clips, an eraser, keys, coins, a candle, cutlery, silver cooking foil, and pieces of glass, wood, paper and plastic. Next take a magnet and gently move it through the pile. It picks up only certain objects and always leaves others.

✴ A magnet attracts mainly objects made of the metals iron, nickel and cobalt, which are magnetic. Other materials are non-magnetic. The magnet picks up objects like pins, nails and paper clips because they are made of steel, which contains iron.

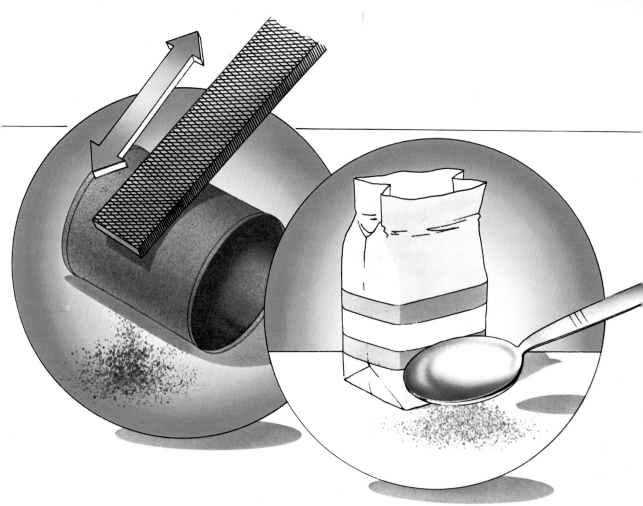

Rust remover

Use a file to scrape some rust from an old
can. Pound it to dust with the back of a
spoon, and mix the rust powder
thoroughly with some sugar. Now separate
this mixture by slowly moving a magnet
through it. The rust particles cling to the
magnet, leaving the sugar behind.

The rust particles contain iron and are
therefore magnetic. As sugar is non-
magnetic, the magnet picks up only the
rust. Magnetic filters are used to purify oil
and other materials in this way.

△ Notice how the rust
particles cling to the
ends of the magnet.
This is where the
magnet's force is
strongest. Any dark bits
left behind are probably
dirt and not rust.

The action of magnets

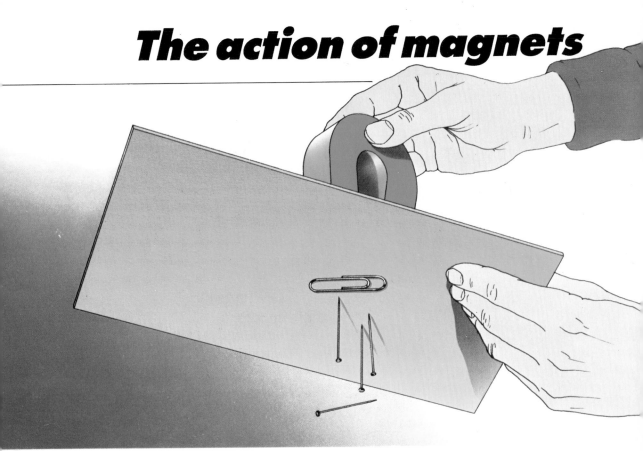

△ The ability of a magnet to attract objects depends on how strong the magnet is and how far away it is from the object. Its field gets weaker as the distance increases. The pins or clips stick to the cardboard because the field penetrating the cardboard is strong enough to hold them up. But as the magnet is moved away, the field gets weaker. When the force becomes less than the weight of the pins or clips, they fall.

How far can a magnet's power extend?

Penetrating power

Spread some pins or paper clips on a table. Hold a piece of cardboard over them. Lower a magnet towards the cardboard. As the magnet comes closer to the cardboard, the pins or clips jump up and cling to it. Raise the magnet and they fall away.

✳ A magnetic field around the magnet gives it power. The field is a region of invisible force that attracts objects made of magnetic materials. The magnetic field goes through non-magnetic materials.

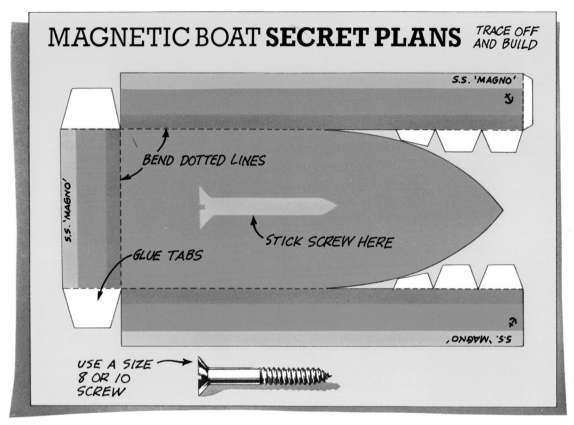

MAGNETIC BOAT **SECRET PLANS** TRACE OFF AND BUILD

S.S. 'MAGNO'

BEND DOTTED LINES

S.S. 'MAGNO'

STICK SCREW HERE

GLUE TABS

S.S. 'MAGNO'

USE A SIZE 8 OR 10 SCREW

Magic boat

Make a small boat out of card as shown and tape a medium-size screw underneath it. Float the boat on some water in a shallow dish placed on a thin tabletop. Make the boat skim over the water and turn in any direction – as if by magic. To do this, conceal a strong magnet beneath the tabletop and move it under the boat.

▽ If the magnet is not strong enough to move the boat, raise the dish on some books and hold the magnet under the dish. Do not use a steel dish.

✸ The magnetic field of the magnet penetrates the tabletop, dish and water. It makes the screw line up with the ends of the magnet, causing the boat to move and turn.

Magnetic poles

Every magnet has two poles. Discover which one is which and how they affect other magnets.

A compass needle points north because it is a magnet.

Pole finder

Suspend a magnet with a piece of cotton so that it hangs freely. Leave it to stop swinging. Turn it slightly and let go. It always comes to a stop with one end pointing north and the other south. Mark the ends N and S to show which is which.

※ The force of a magnet comes from two points inside the ends of the magnet. These are the magnet's poles. They are called the north and south poles. The Earth's magnetic field makes the magnet turn so that the north pole points north and the south pole points south.

△ Make sure that no large pieces of metal such as stoves or refrigerators are nearby as they may cause the magnet to swing away from north and south.

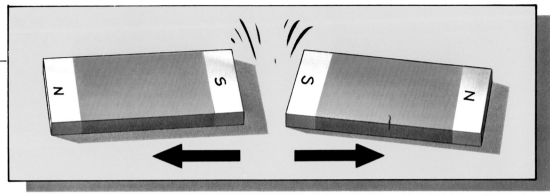

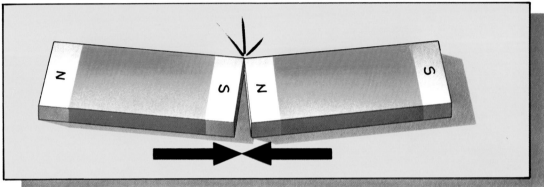

Pushing and pulling

Take another magnet and mark its poles as described in the previous experiment. Now try putting two north poles or two south poles together. A strong force between the magnets tries to push them apart. Turn one magnet round and move a north pole towards a south pole. The magnetic force now pulls the two magnets together.

△ If you know the poles of one magnet, you can find the poles of another by seeing which poles attract one another and which repel.

Two unlike poles – one north and one south – always attract each other. Two like poles – two north poles or two south poles – always repel each other. The force gets stronger as the two poles get closer together.

Fields of force

See the field of invisible force that surrounds a magnet.

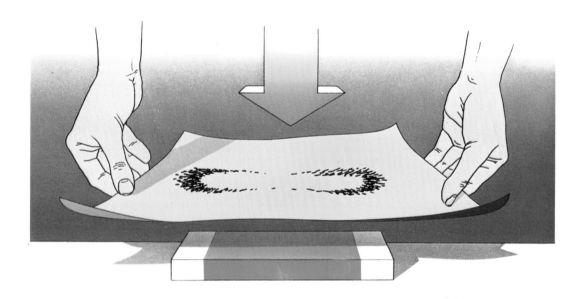

Unlike poles

Hold a sheet of paper over a magnet lying on a table. If you have a horseshoe magnet, support it so that the ends are upright. Now take some iron filings and sprinkle them evenly on the paper. As the filings fall, they move into a pattern of curved lines.

✳ The pattern shows the shape of the magnetic field produced by the magnet. The field consists of lines of force that attract the filings, moving them so that

△ Make some iron filings by holding a big nail in a pair of pliers, and then scraping it with a large file. Use an old pepper pot to sprinkle the filings on the paper. You can preserve the pattern of lines by gently spraying the filings with hair lacquer.

they mark out the field. The magnetic force is strongest where the lines are closest together. The lines of force extend from one pole to the other because the poles are unlike.

Like poles

Repeat the previous experiment, but this time fix two magnets to the table so that two like poles (two north or two south poles) are near each other. The pattern of lines is very different.

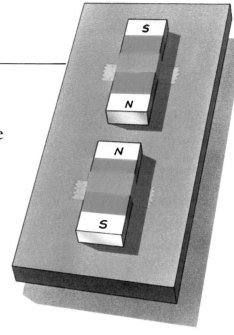

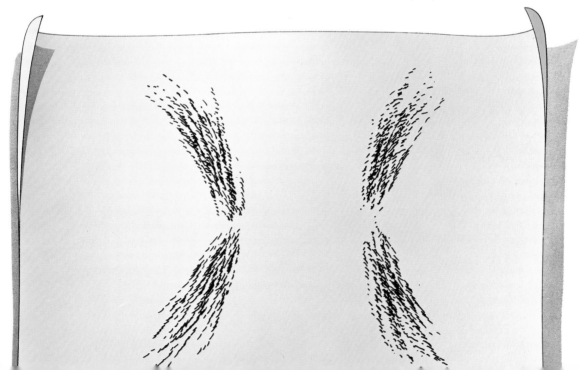 Because the two poles repel each other, their magnetic fields keep apart. The lines of force in the two fields curve away from each other.

△ Use sticky tape to fix the magnets and stop them pushing themselves apart.

▽ Lines of force from the same pole or from two like poles always keep apart.

The magnetic compass

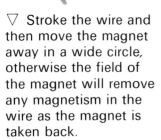

tape   cork

Make a compass and see how sensitive it is to magnetic fields.

North

▽ Stroke the wire and then move the magnet away in a wide circle, otherwise the field of the magnet will remove any magnetism in the wire as the magnet is taken back.

Floating compass

Straighten a paper clip and stick a small piece of tape to one end. Fix the wire to a piece of cork. Then slowly run the south pole of a magnet along the wire towards the marked end as shown. Do this about 30 times, always moving the magnet in the same direction. Float the cork in a dish of water. It comes to rest with the marked end of the wire pointing north.

✸ Stroking the wire with one pole of a magnet in the same direction makes the wire into a weak magnet. The magnet's field produces a north pole at the marked end of the wire, so it always turns to north.

Magnetic detector

Bring a magnet slowly towards the compass. See how the wire moves when the magnet is still some distance away. Now test some steel objects like scissors or cutlery. The compass will indicate whether they are slightly magnetized or not.

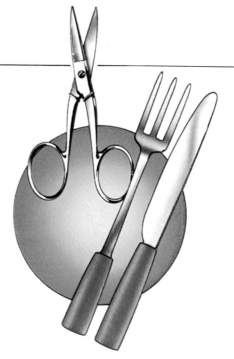

※ The compass swings round to point along the lines of force of any magnetic field. The wire is very light and can move easily. It can therefore detect weak magnetic fields such as the Earth's magnetism. Steel objects may have become slightly magnetized if they have been near strong magnets. The compass is sensitive enough to register their magnetism.

▽ Note that the north end of the compass moves towards the south pole of a magnet or magnetic object and away from the north pole.

The power of attraction

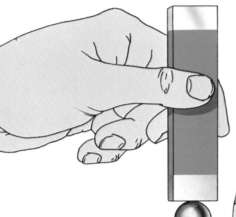

See how magnets can attract objects and produce magnets.

△ You can use pins or paper clips if you do not have any ball bearings, but check first that they are not already magnetized.

Magnetic chains

Take some small ball bearings. Check that they do not attract one another and therefore are not magnetized. Now attach one to the pole of a magnet and hang other bearings from it in a chain. Then carefully detach the first bearing from the magnet. The bearings still hang in a chain. Raise the magnet, and they soon begin to fall off.

✳ The chain of bearings is held in the magnetic field around the magnet. The bearings concentrate the field so that it is strong enough to support them. Raising the magnet spreads out the field until it can no longer hold the bearings.

Magnets make magnets

Take a pin and place its head on the north pole of a magnet. Then test its magnetism with the floating compass shown on page 14. Note that the head of the pin is a south pole, and that the point is north. Next place the head of the same pin on the south pole of the magnet. Test it again; the head is now north and the point south.

✳ When a magnet attracts an object such as the pin, it magnetizes it. The field around the pole of the magnet produces an unlike pole in the nearest part of the object, the head. A little magnetism then remains in the pin, but the poles are easily changed by the strong field of the magnet.

▽ Bring the pin close to the compass to test its magnetism.

17

Magnets can push

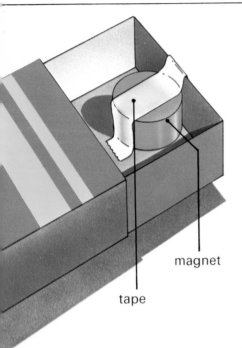

magnet

tape

Magnets can make objects float above the ground or force each other aside.

Hovering matchbox

Take two matchboxes. Stick a small magnet in one box and tape it to the tabletop as shown. Then stick another magnet in the other box. Hold it under the first box so that like poles face each other. The first box will hover above the other box, moving gently up and down as if suspended from an invisible spring.

▽ It helps to hinge the first box to the tabletop with some sticky tape to stop the box from being pushed to one side.

✹ The two magnets in the matchboxes repel each other because like poles are placed together. The first box rises until the force between the magnets is equal to the weight of the box.

tape hinge

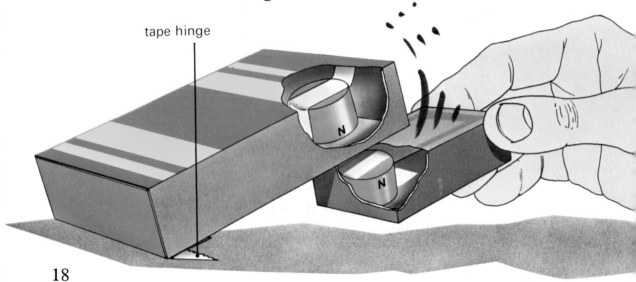

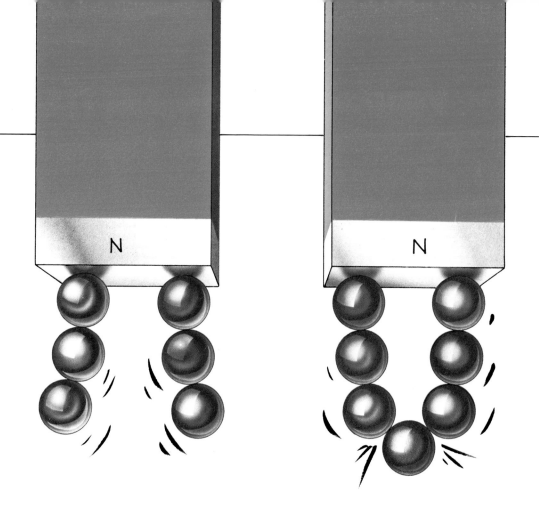

Keeping apart – and together

Build up two chains of ball bearings on one pole of a magnet as shown. The two chains will tend to push each other apart. Now bring up another ball bearing between the two chains. Both chains are attracted to the bearing and form a loop.

✻ The two chains normally force each other apart because they are both attached to the same pole of the magnet. However, the bearings stick together in chains because they shorten the lines of force in the magnetic field. The extra ball does this for both chains and so attracts them both.

△ This experiment can be done with pins if you do not have any ball bearings.

Vanishing magnetism

Magnetism can be made to disappear for a time or it may be lost entirely.

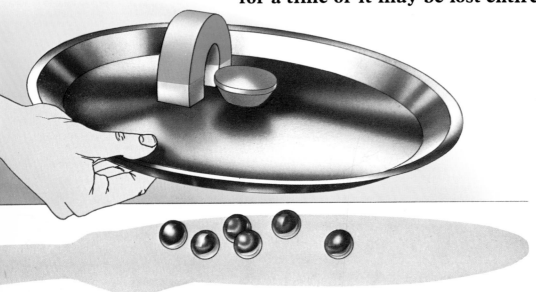

Cut off a magnetic field

Take some steel objects like ball bearings. Check that they are attracted to a magnet, but do not attract each other. Attach the magnet to the upper side of a wide steel plate. Then lower the plate over the bearings as shown. The magnet will not now pick up the bearings.

✳ The field of the magnet goes into the steel plate and does not pass through it. The plate therefore cuts off the field so that the magnet cannot pick up the bearings.

△ Objects made of magnetic materials like steel affect the field of a magnet. The lines of force curve into the object, the field's shape depending on the power of the magnet and size of the object. This experiment therefore may not work if the magnet is very strong. It also depends on the thickness and metal of the plate.

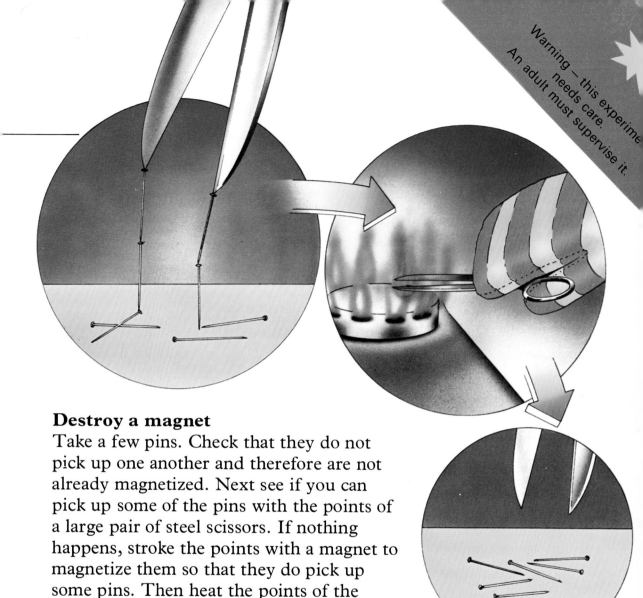

Destroy a magnet

Take a few pins. Check that they do not pick up one another and therefore are not already magnetized. Next see if you can pick up some of the pins with the points of a large pair of steel scissors. If nothing happens, stroke the points with a magnet to magnetize them so that they do pick up some pins. Then heat the points of the scissors red-hot in a gas burner. Cool them by plunging the points in water, wipe them dry and test them again. Now the scissors will not pick up any pins.

Heating a magnet like this destroys its magnetism. Inside a magnet, tiny regions of magnetism are lined up like rows of miniature magnets. Heating makes them move out of line, removing the magnetism.

△ Take great care not to burn yourself when you heat the scissors to remove their magnetism. Hold them in an oven glove. A fork or screwdriver may work if you have no large scissors.

Strange effects

The magnetic fields around magnets can behave in unusual ways and cause mysterious things to happen.

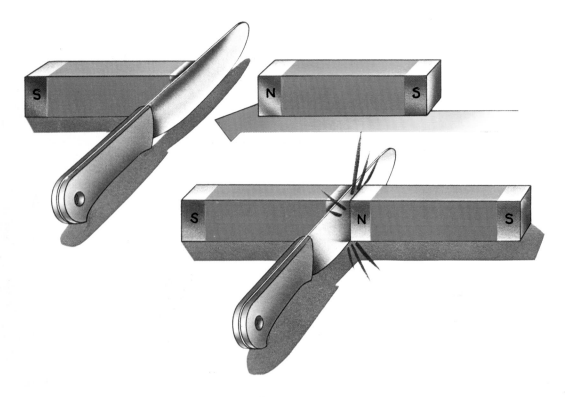

△ The knife blade should be quite long for this experiment to work.

Fair share

Take a bar magnet and attach a wide but thin steel object to one pole. A knife blade will do. Next take another magnet and find which end has the same pole. Ask a friend to guess whether this pole will attract or repel the object. (Remember that like poles are involved.) Then bring up the magnet. It is attracted. Turn one magnet round and try again. The two magnets are always attracted, no matter which poles are on either side of the object.

✺ The poles of both magnets attract the object and try to share it between them, thus holding the two magnets together. Inside the object the fields of the two magnets make the tiny regions of magnetism turn and line up in different directions. On one side they point toward the magnet on that side; on the other side of the object the regions point toward the other magnet.

Dividing the spoils

Repeat the previous experiment but this time use two steel objects. Will the like poles of the two magnets still be attracted? In fact, the two objects leap apart.

✺ Both poles pull in opposite directions. As the two objects can move apart, each magnet pulls one of the objects toward it. If you could cut through the knife blade in the previous experiment, this is what would happen.

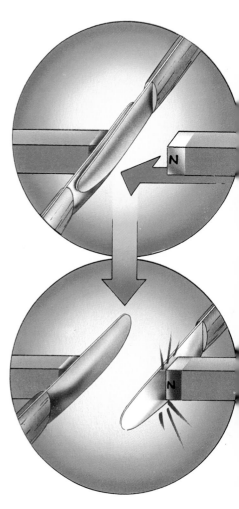

△ Choose steel objects that are sufficiently thin for both to stick to the first magnet.

Continued over page

Wriggling ball

Repeat the experiment on page 22 again, but this time with a small ball bearing. Will the two magnets still come together? In fact, the ball tries to wriggle out of the way.

 The lines of force in the first magnet's field normally keep the ball bearing in the center of the face of the first magnet. But as the other magnet approaches, the lines from both poles force each other apart. The ball bearing tries to shorten the lines of force, which it can now do more at the edge of the magnet. It therefore rolls away from the center.

▽ As it is free to move, the ball bearing will always roll to the place at which the magnetic field is strongest. This is the point at which it can most shorten the lines of force.

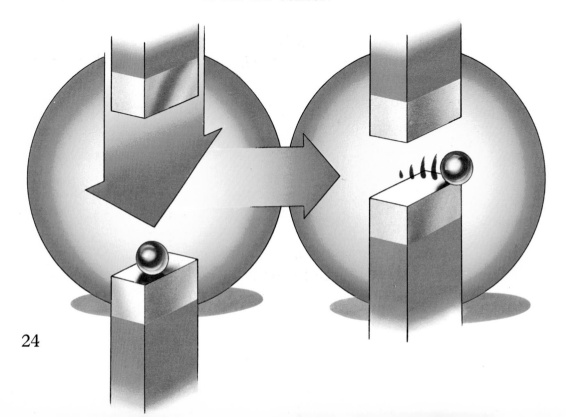

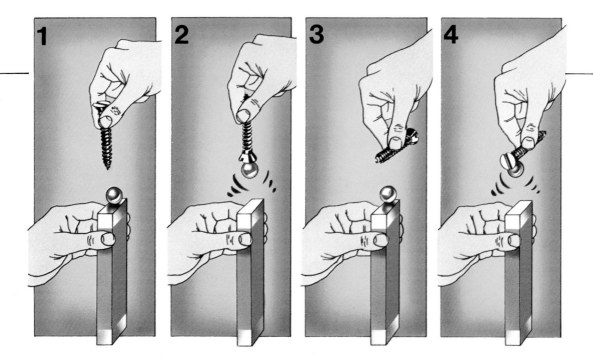

Transfer of power

Could an object like a screw be more powerful than a magnet? Take a magnet and a ball bearing. Find a long screw with a head about the same width as the bearing. First make sure that the bearing and screw do not attract one another. Then place the bearing on one pole of the magnet. Hold the magnet and try to pick up the ball with the screw in various positions. Sometimes the bearing is picked up, sometimes not.

✳ The position of the screw affects the magnetic field of the magnet. The ball bearing moves to the place in which it can most shorten the lines of force in the field and is held there.

△ **1** The point of the screw does not lift the ball.
2 The head of the screw does raise it.
3 The narrow end does not attract the ball.
4 The wide end does attract it.

This experiment works with all kinds of magnets and objects made of steel or other magnetic metals. However, the result depends on the power of the magnet, and on the size, shape and position of the objects. Try different objects in several positions and see what happens.

25

Magnetism and electricity

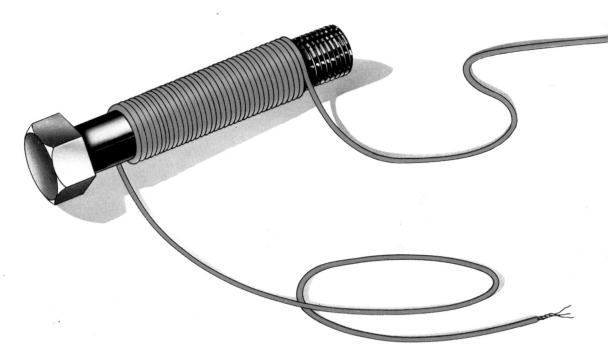

△ Wind as many turns
of wire around the bolt
as possible. If necessary,
use sticky tape to stop
the wire from coming
off the bolt. The bulb in
the lamp holder should
be the same voltage as
the battery.

Build an electromagnet

Take a steel bolt about $\frac{5}{8}$ in across and
4 in long and check that it is not
magnetized by testing it with the floating
compass described on page 14. Then wind
some wire covered with plastic insulation
around the bolt. Use the thinnest wire you
can find, and always wind it in the same
direction around the bolt. Connect the ends
of the wire to a battery – 4.5 volts should

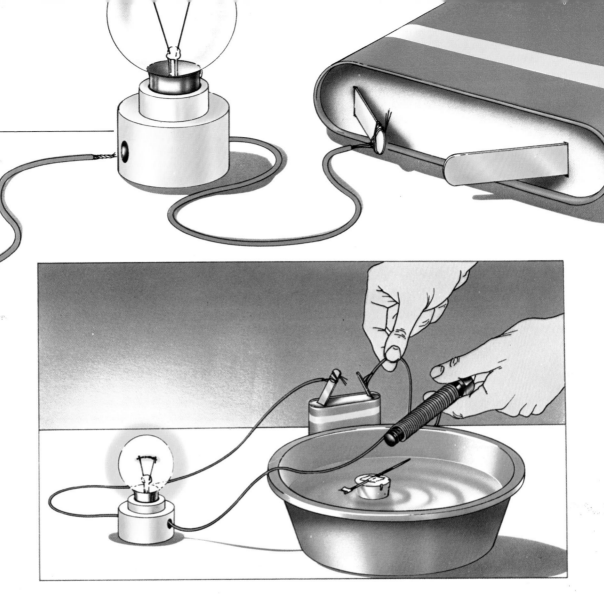

do – and a lamp holder as shown. Place the bolt near the compass and notice that whenever the bulb lights up, the compass swings.

✳ Winding the wire around the bolt turns it into an electromagnet. The coil of wire produces a magnetic field when the current flows. The bolt concentrates this field so that it acts like the field of a bar magnet.

△ Touch the free end of the wire to the battery to make the electromagnet work. The bulb lights up to show that electricity is flowing through the electromagnet and magnetizing it.

Continued *over page*

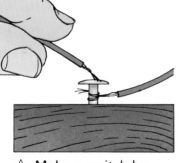

△ Make a switch by pushing two drawing pins into a piece of board and connecting the wires from the bolt to them. Then connect two more wires to the battery terminals. Press the ends of these wires on the drawing pins to make the electromagnet work. Swap the wires over to change the terminals.

Switching poles

Place the electromagnet described on page 26 near the floating compass. Connect it to the battery with a simple switch as shown so that the terminals can be easily changed. See how the compass swings to and fro as you switch the terminals.

✹ The compass moves to and fro because the poles of the electromagnet change from north to south or south to north and back again. This is because the poles depend on which way the current flows around the coil of wire. Changing the terminals reverses the flow of current. Electric motors turn electricity into movement in a similar way.

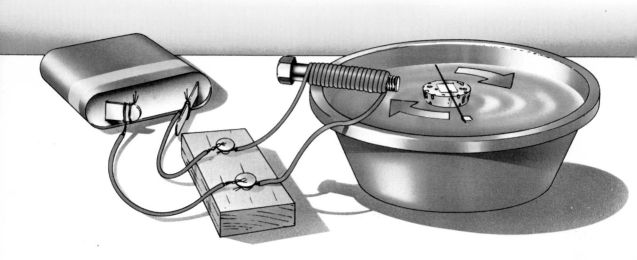

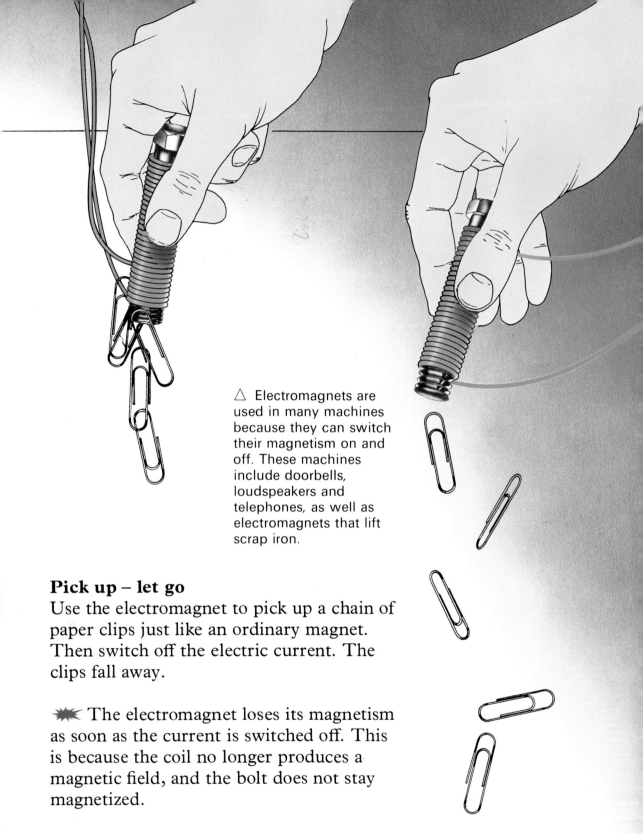

△ Electromagnets are used in many machines because they can switch their magnetism on and off. These machines include doorbells, loudspeakers and telephones, as well as electromagnets that lift scrap iron.

Pick up – let go

Use the electromagnet to pick up a chain of paper clips just like an ordinary magnet. Then switch off the electric current. The clips fall away.

The electromagnet loses its magnetism as soon as the current is switched off. This is because the coil no longer produces a magnetic field, and the bolt does not stay magnetized.

More about magnetism

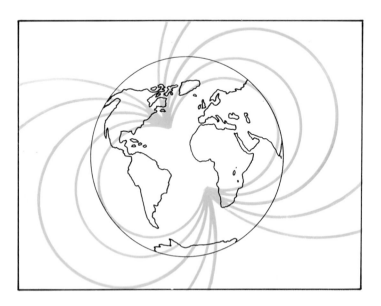

Electric motor
A simple electric motor contains a magnet and a coil of wire. Electricity passes through the wire and makes it a second magnet. The magnetic fields of the coil and magnet push and pull on each other. This causes either the coil or the magnet to turn. The current is constantly switched from positive to negative in such a way that the motor continues to turn.

Earth's magnetism
The Earth is magnetic. It has a magnetic field that extends all over the Earth's surface and out into space. The field acts as if there is a huge magnet within the Earth. The north pole of the Earth's magnetic field is below Antarctica near the South Pole. The south pole of this field is beneath the Arctic near the North Pole. This is why a magnetic compass points towards north. However, it does not always point directly north because the Earth's

△ The lines of force in the Earth's magnetic field run from its south pole to its north pole. A compass needle turns until it points along a line of force.

magnetic field does not line up exactly with the true North and South Poles. The difference is called magnetic variation, and it is different in different places. Local maps give the variation. The Earth's magnetism is possibly caused by huge electric currents deep inside the Earth.

Magnetic trains
The most advanced kinds of trains are powered by magnetism. Instead of having wheels, powerful magnetic fields produced by electro-magnets in the train and along the track support the train just above the track. The magnetic fields also push or pull on the train to move it along the track. Because they are not in contact with the track, magnetic trains can travel much faster than ordinary trains and are very much quieter.

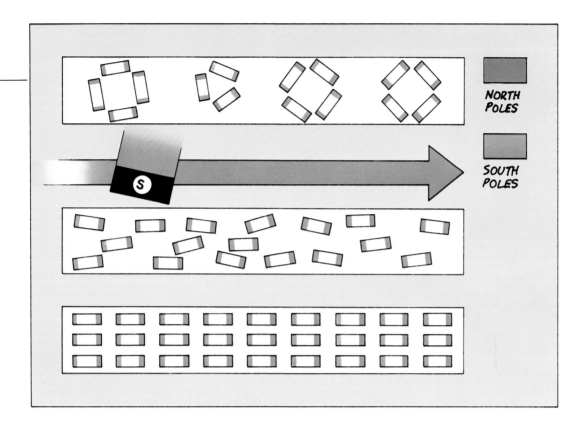

NORTH POLES

SOUTH POLES

△ The tiny regions of magnetism within a magnetic material normally form closed chains so that the material has no overall magnetic field. When it is magnetized, the regions all line up so their poles face in the same direction.

Magnetism

Inside a magnetic material like iron or steel, there are many tiny regions of magnetism. These have north and south poles and are like very tiny magnets.

Normally, the regions all lie in different directions. Their magnetic fields cancel each other out, so the piece of material does not have a magnetic field overall. If a strong magnetic field comes from outside, all the regions line up so that their poles point in the same direction. This can be done by placing the material in an electric coil or by stroking it with a strong magnet. The tiny magnetic fields now add up to give the material a magnetic field overall. The piece of

material becomes magnetic. When the outside field is removed, the regions may move back out of line and the material loses its magnetism. This happens with pure iron. But with some materials, including kinds of steel, the regions stay lined up. The piece of material has become a permanent magnet. Heating it or subjecting it to a rapidly changing magnetic field is necessary to move the magnetic regions and make it lose its magnetism.

Index